Gems Along the Way

Wayne Cordeiro

GEMS ALONG THE WAY

Published by New Hope Resources
© 1997 by Wayne Cordeiro.
ISBN 0-9654251-0-X

Scripture taken from the NEW AMERICAN STANDARD BIBLE ®, © The Lockman Foundation 1960, 1962, 1963, 1968, 1971, 1972, 1973, 1975, 1977.
Used by permission.

Executive Editor: Carole Ka'apu

Staff Editors: Beth Naholowaa Murph, Steffany Shima, Scott and Sandi Tompkins

Design & Layout: Bernie Kim

Cover Art: Jan Shima & Bernie Kim

Mahalo to those who have helped with this project:

Tammy Aguiar, Fran Hesterman, Kathy Lee, Shery Matsumoto, John & Joanne McCollum, and Pam Thomas.

For information contact:

New Hope Resources
290 Sand Island Access Rd.
Honolulu, HI 96819
www.newhope-hawaii.org

Printed in the United States of America.

Table of Contents

Acknowledgments

These gems were found along the way over a period of fifteen years. The lessons I was learning, I wanted to give to my children, but at the time of discovery, they were too young to understand. I didn't want to lose the memory of these gems, so I kept a journal to record them as they were being delivered. This is the first journal of the gems I found along the way.

I want to thank the many people who have been such an integral part of my growth. No one can solo through life without some irreplaceable friendships along the way. Over the years, many have become not only friends, but family.

Sometimes I wish my mom were still alive so I could thank her in person because her touch on my life left an indelible mark of love and support. She would often sing me to sleep and although a single mom, she sacrificed with gladness so that her kids would not have to go without their needs being met. We always had enough because she cared.

Thank you Pauline Spencer for your support even when we went through storms. To Doris Aoki and Noel Campbell, Ed Nakamoto, and Sam Shim, who have taught me how to encourage others by their constant example. To the wonderful staff of New Hope Hilo and New Hope Oʻahu for their willingness to pick up a paddle and stroke as a team. To Dan and Carol

Ann Shima who have helped me to care for my family more through their unselfish caring for me. Thank you to Ron and Mo Bright for their role in raising such wonderful kids. You are an example to us all. To our leaders and volunteers at New Hope, and to the wonderful Foursquare family that I belong to. It is such a joy to take the Good News to the ends of the earth!

A final and special Thank You to my family: Anna, Amy, Aaron and Abby, who are and will always be my first pastorate. I write these with much love, with the heart of a father, the ears of a listener, from the hands of a learner, and through the eyes of reflection.

—Wayne Cordeiro

Dedication

To Anna,

Thank you for the wonderful way you love our family as well as your husband. I am humbled every time I think of all the ways you support and encourage us. You know each of us intimately, including our weaknesses, yet you are always believing in us and thinking the best of us.

Your unconditional love has been one of the single most important influences in my life. It has helped me to become a man of God, not just in public and but more so in private. Sometimes I feel so inadequate and so ill equipped, yet your love and support give me room to grow. One of the best ways I sense your support is by you daily ushering me before Jesus so I will learn and be changed into His image. As a result, I live in the constant realization of how much I am loved.

You are and always have been an integral part of my ministry. You may not be up on the platform with me physically, but you are always there. And with your love and encouragement, I can share the Word the rest of my life because of a lovely woman who chose to support God's call on my life, and who chose to share her life with me when we were still in Bible College. You have been my inspiration and without your patience and love, I would never have had the time to find the gems along the way.

I love you so very much,
Wayne

Gems for
Family and Friends

Love of Choice

*Always remember that a love of
choice is the most powerful love
of all.*

Dear Abby,

You just turned one month old, and every
time I look at you, my heart feels as if it will
burst with love. I still remember the day we saw
you. You were only three days old. You
immediately became such a special part of our
family. You will always remind me of how much
Jesus loves me.

In John 15:16, He says, "You did not choose
Me, but I chose you, and appointed you, that
you should go and bear fruit, and that your fruit
should remain..."

Before you were even born your Mom and I
chose you. Sometimes when a mother gets
pregnant, she feels she doesn't have much of a
choice — but we did. Before we ever saw you, we
loved you. Before we knew whether you would
be a girl or boy, we wanted you. Before we knew
whether or not you'd be healthy, we were
committed to you.

When I think of you, I think of Jesus and how He loves me. His love has nothing to do with my looks, my height, my health, or my background. He chose to love me, and He chose me to be one of His "adopted" kids. He chose me!

Some would have you believe that being adopted makes us "second class" citizens. But the fact is that it really makes us "first class" because we are especially chosen. We've received God's wonderful love of choice!

Always remember that a love of choice is the most powerful love of all. God calls it an "agape" love. That's the kind of love He has for us, and that's the kind I have for you. That kind of love requires commitment and it costs a lot . . . but you're worth it!

I'm so proud of you Sweetheart.

With all my love,
Dad

Friendship

*One of the best ways to be a good
friend is to be an encourager.*

Dear Amy, Aaron, and Abby,

Some time ago, I was thinking about who I
would call my closest friends. There are many, but
off the top, I came up with a list of about seven
people. Then I asked myself what made them such
special friends.

The common strand among them was that they
were all encouragers.

They all supported and motivated me. They
spoke God's truth into my life. They kept praying
for me until I received the fullness of the Lord's
promises. They were people with whom I could
bare my thoughts. I knew they would receive the
outpourings of my heart — the "grain and chaff
together" — and sift it with gentlest of hands,
blow away that which was not worth keeping, and
return to me the best of the grain.

God values friendship so much that He
mentions it over a hundred times in the Bible.
Friendship is part of His plan for our spiritual and
emotional growth. That's why Jesus sent His
disciples out two-by-two. He knew the Gospel
would be understood best in the context of
relationships. Later on in John 17, He prayed for

His disciples to be united in friendship. He prayed that we'd be one so that the world would believe! It is in our friendships that Jesus would be seen as credible to the world! That's incredible!

I hope you find good friends. But beware! Friendship is something like happiness. The more you seek after it, the more slippery and elusive it becomes. The first step in finding good friends is to be one. Dale Carnegie once said, "You can make more friends in two months by becoming interested in others than in two years by trying to get others interested in you!" We all need love and acceptance, and when we give it to others, it usually comes back to us in some way.

One of the best ways to be a good friend is to be an encourager. When I saw the impact of encouragement in my life, I thought, "If that's what makes them such good friends, I want to become an encourager too!"

Be an encourager. Train your eyes to see what is good about people, and tell them! Think of it this way. Just imagine that around the neck of every person you come in contact with hangs a large sign. On it is written: "Please make me feel valuable."

Tell them how valuable they are. You see, when people feel valuable when they are around you, they will define you as a "friend."

Jesus is like that, isn't He? That is why we find in John, "No longer do I call you slaves,... but I [call] you friends..." (Jn. 15:15).

Your friend,
Dad

Accepting God's Placement

God never makes mistakes with His placement. When we make decisions based on what we know, regardless of how we feel, we move towards wisdom and joy.

Dear Amy, Aaron, and Abby,

When I flew in from Tulsa, Oklahoma, tonight I was so tired. Yet the instant I saw you all at the airport my spirits began to rise. It reminded me again how much I love the family the Lord has given me. I guess he could have placed me with any other family in another state or even in another era, but in His wisdom, He placed me here. God knows what He's doing!

Of course, our family is by no means perfect. There may be times when you'll feel like you'd be better off in another family. You may see that other kids have more privileges, more material things, or more freedom. You'll look at your boundaries in comparison to others, and you'll feel like you're "losing out." You'll want more latitude, more "say" in how things are done.

I understand how you might feel each of these things. But when all these emotions come crashing down upon you at once remember: always go back to what you know, not what you feel. God never makes mistakes with His placement. When we make decisions based on what we know, regardless of how we feel, we move towards wisdom and joy. Making decisions on feelings moves us toward anger, bitterness, and insecurity.

God put us together for a very eternal reason. Whatever you feel, know that I love you dearly. Though our shortcomings can be very obvious at times, don't ever let them invalidate God's will. Come talk with me, and we'll go to Jesus together. I would consider it a privilege to have your company as we stand before the throne as people who are . . .

> Growing together,
> Your Dad

Seeking God's Best

*Seek God's ways and pray for
someone who does the same.*

My dear Amy,

Soon you'll be noticing boys, and hoping they'll notice you! (A silent prayer is offered here.) This is all a natural part of growing up, hormone changes, and a desire for acceptance from the opposite sex. There will be some boys who will appreciate your inner qualities of kindness, grace, and friendliness. However, other boys will only appreciate your physical beauty.

You'll have a tendency to pay attention to the boys who pay attention to you, but never respond only to these. Be careful and watch over your heart! The emotional web is constructed with very strong fibers, and each one you spin takes three times as long to un-spin! That's why I suggest that you not "go steady" in high school. It can lead to needless heartaches and temptations. Enjoy "brother-sister" relationships instead. And should you go out, only go in groups. Above all, ask God for Christian friends of both sexes.

When you're sizing up a guy, look for strong character qualities. They are far more important than good looks or popularity. Never mind if a guy is wealthy, so long as he is wise. Never mind if he is famous, so long as he is faithful. Sooner or later (Mom and I prefer later), you'll notice a "special" guy. Pray for this one before you even meet him. God will know who he is before you will. Pray for his spiritual growth and maturity. Pray especially that he has a genuine relationship with Jesus.

You might ask, "What's wrong with dating a non-Christian?"

That is an often-asked question. Let me explain it as simply as I can. A non-Christian will be building his life as best he knows how, but when he does, he will do so from a completely different perspective, or blueprint than yours. That's why Paul says in 2 Corinthians 6:14, "Do not be bound together with unbelievers..."

Say for example, if you and a non-Christian were thinking about marriage. You were both fine contractors, so I asked you to build me a house. Now I asked you to start building at one end while he began at the other end. You were going to meet in the middle. The only problem was that each of you were building from a different set of blueprints. Now each of you could be building sincerely, excellently, and you could be doing the best you could. However, when you arrived at the middle, you'd still have to compromise to join the two halves. It would be precisely at the joining of the two halves that, should any strain be put on the house, that's where it would give in!

It's the same way when a Christian marries an unbeliever. The believer is building a marriage from one set of blueprints and while the unbeliever is using another.

Mom and I encourage you to seek God's ways and pray for someone who does the same. Then your relationship will be pleasing to God (and us). That's what your Mom did . . . and look how happy she is!

"Humbly" yours,
Dad

The Value of a Mother's Love!

*I thank God for a sensitive Mom
who knows Jesus in such a way
that she can accompany you to
the throne of the King.*

My dear son Aaron,

Yesterday you asked Mom what would happen if you died.

"Would you have a funeral and then bury me?"

"Yes," she replied with obvious concern in her voice.

"Will I go to heaven?"

"Yes," she replied.

"How will I know that for sure?"

"Because the Bible says that if you believe in Jesus, ask for forgiveness, and receive Him as Lord, you will be saved." (You have a smart Mom!)

"What should I tell Jesus right now to let Him know I really want to go to heaven?"

At that point you prayed, asked Jesus into your heart, and let Him be Lord of your life. I'm so glad you did. Each of us must make that decision, and I thank God for a sensitive Mom who knows Jesus in such a way that she can accompany you to the throne of the King!

Pray for your mom. She knows Jesus very well, and as she's walking through life with you, she can tell you lots more about Him.

Don't ever let the devil drive a wedge between you and her. And don't ever take her for granted. (That's usually the first signs of a wedge.) Aside from the Lord, she's one of the most important influences in your life. Let her know that — today. Let her know you care — today. She's been doing that for you non-stop since the day you were born.

Thanking Jesus for you and Mom!
Dad

*G*ems for
Listening to God

Learning to Hear

God will always be speaking,
and to hear Him, we must bend
our ear to hear the vibrations of
His heart.

Dear Aaron,

Today I am in Portland, Oregon where I'll be speaking at a youth conference. There are a lot of high schoolers here, and many of them don't know Jesus... at least not yet!

Earlier today while I was tuning my guitar, the soundman cranked up some ear-piercing rock music, the kind that makes you feel your heartbeat with each thump of the kick drum. I kept trying to tune my guitar by putting my ear closer and closer to it, but to no avail. My acoustic Martin guitar was no match for the high powered speakers. Finally, I had to resort to placing my ear right onto the wood itself. Then lo and behold, regardless of how loud the music raged, I could still hear my Martin . . . not because my acoustic guitar got any louder, but because my ear got closer!

In Deuteronomy 6:4, God says, "Hear, O Israel. . ." In the New Testament, Jesus echoed this verse with the phrase, "He who has ears to hear, let him hear" (Mark 4:9, Luke 8:8, 14:35).

Aaron, you'll come to times when the voices around you are so loud that it will be difficult to hear the gentle voice of the Lord. Yes, He can speak in thunderous ways too, but that wouldn't require any faith to hear that. God could do some handwriting on the wall, but that wouldn't please Him, either. Again, it would require no faith on our part in obeying.

In Hebrews 11:6, it tells us, "Without faith, it is impossible to please [God]."

God will always be speaking, but sometimes in order to hear Him, we must bend our ears to hear the very vibrations of His heart. We can't "turn off" the music nor amplify His voice, but if we let our ears touch Him and bend ourselves before Him, we will hear. Someone once told me, "If you're going to bow, bow low. Then you will hear not only His voice, but you'll hear His heart as well."

So I've learned over the years that in walking with the King, bow low. That's right. Don't stop till you hear the very vibrations of His heart. Don't just pretend to know Him. Take the time to REALLY know Him by listening for His heart.

I think that's what really pleases God. He doesn't want us to expect His voice to always be loud and booming. Instead, He wants us to be a people who are willing to simply bend our ears to touch Him. What pleases Him are people who are willing to take the time to listen.

Developing ears that hear,
Dad

Responding With Righteousness

*"Never despise anything that takes
you to your knees."*—Ron Mehl

Dear Amy, Aaron, and Abby,

I'm not really excited about flying anymore. I used to be, but it gets rather tiring. Yesterday, due to some heavy fog, we landed in Oakland instead of San Francisco. The fuel truck stalled before getting to the plane, and we ended up waiting in the plane for three hours on the runway.

I heard a lot of people grumbling. Some of them seemed to be ready to explode. I felt the same way, too! But just as I was ready to pull the pin and let one of the flight attendants in on my displeasure, I heard the words of James 1:19-20 ringing in my ears.

"But let everyone be quick to hear, slow to speak and slow to anger; for the anger of man does not achieve the righteousness of God."

So instead of sending shrapnel throughout the fuselage, I spent the time reading the Bible and praying for you, for Mom, the church. I even prayed for the flight attendants that had to deal with all the other malcontents on the plane.

Although I disliked the inconvenience, I liked the opportunity for character growth that it provided for me. A good friend of mine, Ron Mehl, once said, "Never despise anything that takes you to your knees."

You will be faced with some terrible and unfair situations, but instead of letting them control you (that's what Satan wants), let them take you to your knees (that's what God wants). God is able, and He has always been faithful to bring me through every negative situation. When I let God deal with my struggle rather than the devil, I come through with more character and likeness. Then when we come out the other side, we'll arrive better, and not bitter!

Growing on my knees,
Dad

"Tuning In" to the Lord

*If I fight against God's voice
hard enough, it will dull my
ears. If I love His voice and
respond to it, it will always be
clear and distinct.*

Dear Amy,

We recently moved into our little house in
Hilo. It's a peaceful neighborhood except for a
frustrated dog who loves to hear his own bark.
He starts his annoying tirade at 9:30 p.m. sharp
and ends at 5 a.m. About the time I get up from
a sleepless night, he'd curl up and go to sleep! At
first, I was so irritated that I began to think of
ways to quietly and effectively put that creature
out of its misery. But after hurling a few rocks
and angry words at him, I got the frustration out
of my system and gave the situation over to the Lord.

Time slowly slipped by and I began getting
used to this "mad dog." Then, after a few
months slipped by, I didn't hear the dog
anymore (unless someone brought the irritation
to my attention.) It has become commonplace
to me. I guess I've gotten numb to it. It's
amazing what a little time will do. On the other
hand, Abby is now over a year old. She still cries
at night. But even though she's been making

noises at night since she was born, it's never become "commonplace" to your mother. Mom wakes up out of a deep sleep at Abby's first cry in the middle of the night . . . well, most of the time. She can pick out the sound of Abby's voice in a nursery full of screaming babies. Your mother has not allowed Abby's (or Aaron's or your) cries to become commonplace, so they move her to action every time.

I wonder if we make God's voice more like a dog's bark or a baby's cry? If I fight against God's voice hard enough, I will dull my ears to it. If I love His voice and respond to it, it will always be clear and distinct. I'll hear His voice in the night, in a crowd of people, in the middle of the world, or at two in the morning.

When God speaks, don't throw stones or allow His voice to become commonplace. If you do, He'll keep talking, but you won't be able to hear Him anymore. So keep . . .

Listening,
Dad

How Many Times?

Listen carefully to what Jesus is saying.

My dear son Aaron,

For some time now, I've been telling you not to rub your eyes with dirty hands. Well, you did, and your eyes became red and infected. When I saw you, I was so exasperated. "How many times does your father have to tell you something before you listen?!" I screamed.

I guess you've heard that question a lot over the years. Well recently, I found out how unpleasant it is to be scolded that way. You know how often I've encouraged people to pray. Yet in the midst of our busy summer schedule, I found I was praying very little. On three different occasions the Lord challenged me to get back on track with my prayer life. Each time, I was duly convicted and determined to get back into a routine of daily prayer, but I could never seem to get back on schedule.

Finally, I was golfing one day with another pastor. He said, "You know, I heard that the ministers of growing churches pray on the average of 45 minutes a day, but the pastors of mediocre ones pray on the average of only three minutes a day." At that moment, it was as if the

Father's voice split the clouds and said, "Wayne, how many times does your Father have to tell you something before you listen?!"

I've really been enjoying my quiet times lately. I'm back in the groove, but the Lord had to break through my dull ears. Listen carefully to what Jesus is saying. Listen closely to His voice. He is giving you directions each and every day.

Learning to listen,
Dad

P.S. . . . and quit rubbing your eyes!

Taking Sabbath Moments

*Sometimes you will feel alone,
but don't let your "aloneness" go
to waste. Let it bring you closer to
the Lord.*

My dear son Aaron,

The last three days I have had a great time camping out at a park on Kauai. My friend and I came here to relax, read our Bibles, and hear God. That doesn't mean we can't hear God while still at home, but sometimes "aloneness" brings "nearness." The absence of people, demands, routines, and phone calls allows me to spend more time with the Lord. He never changes, but sometimes the scenery needs to change so I can see Him more clearly.

Yesterday afternoon, I was sitting on the sand — nothing too exciting about that. But since I had a lot of time, I started looking at it closely. It intrigued me to discover that there were tiny puka-shells everywhere. These beautifully colored shells were there all along, but they were revealed only after I took the time to look closely.

Sometimes you will also feel a need to be alone. But don't let your "aloneness" go to waste. Take time to look and listen for God.

Look for Him in the earth around you. Block out the noise in order to hear His whispers. Quiet the clamor in order to hear His heart. Those kinds of "ears" don't come at birth. They come by asking, then listening — and in the listening, you will find that He gives you ears with which to hear.

Take time to listen, son. You're never alone unless you choose to move away from Jesus. Stay close. Press in. Listen . . . He's speaking.

Epaphtha! ("Be opened!")
Dad

*G*ems for
Drawing Closer to Jesus

Forgotten . . . Begotten

*Your personal relationship with
Jesus is the most important of all.*

Dear Amy,

The other day while we were at the dinner
table, I asked you and Aaron to quote your
favorite Scripture. You said John 3:16 was yours,
so I asked you to say it. You started off pretty
well. You said, "For God so loved the world that
He gave His only forgotten Son ..." Your mother
tried to conceal her laughter, but she didn't succeed.

Although we know it's not "forgotten" but
"begotten," it is still true that Jesus is often God's
"forgotten" Son. Someone once said we could take
Jesus out of half the churches, and they would just
keep on going as if nothing had happened.

If you boiled faith down to its lowest
denominator and eliminated all the religious
trappings, choruses, and church buildings, only
your relationship with Jesus would remain. He alone
is the one irreducible relationship of your faith.

There is a scientific principle that says that if
your basic premise is off, then every conclusion
thereafter will also be off. That holds true not

only in science. If we lose that simple and pure devotion to our relationship with Jesus, then the other conclusions we come to will be inaccurate.

How are you doing with Jesus? Not with church or the Bible . . . but with Jesus? Your personal relationship with Him is the most important of all. He is God's only begotten provision for salvation, forgiveness, and eternal life.

Always remembering,
Dad

Getting to Know Jesus

*The Bible reveals Jesus Christ -
look for Him.*

Dear Amy,

I've been walking with the Lord for sixteen years now, and the more I get to know Him, the more I love Him. But I haven't always had such a close relationship with Him. When I first became a Christian, I knew Jesus only as my Savior. I didn't discover Him as a friend until I began pursuing Him.

Let me give you a little example. Today is Wednesday, so I took the garbage out this morning. Our garbage man comes every Wednesday without fail to pick up our trash. We take this service for granted. Although he's been very regular and faithful to remove even the stinkiest of garbage, we still don't even know his name! What would it take for us to learn his name? Maybe if he not only cleared away our trash, but he also sterilized our garbage cans. Now that would be impressive! Then what if he not only emptied our trash and cleaned the cans, but then he filled them with groceries and money! Would I want to get to know his name now? Why I'd be standing outside each Wednesday morning with a greeting, a smile, and a cup of coffee!

Well, that's exactly how Jesus is!

He's been so faithful to take away the garbage from our hearts. But He didn't stop there! He doesn't just take away our sins (our spiritual garbage) and send us off empty-handed. Every time we bring our garbage to Him, He is so faithful to wash us clean and fill us with His very best. I was always thankful to have my sins forgiven, but it wasn't until I began to experience Jesus' abundant goodness that I really wanted to get to know Him more! I found He was easy to get to know, once I started talking to Him (in prayer) and looking for Him (in the Bible).

Talk with Him often and bring your garbage to Him. He will never refuse you. When you come to Him, you'll never leave the same.

Coming just as I am and leaving more like He is!
Dad

Fixing Our Hope

*When we fix our hope on Him,
we are purified of trivial things
that really aren't important when
compared to our going to heaven!*

Dear Amy and Aaron,

The two of you used to love going to the Kona side of the Big Island of Hawaii because of the white sand beaches. Whenever we would go, we would make a whole day of it with a picnic lunch, swimming, snorkeling, and sunburns. I remember how excited you both were when I announced one Friday that we would be going to Kona after church on Sunday. Both of you jumped up and down and danced to a made-up tune, "Tomorrow we're going to Kona! Tomorrow we're going to Kona!"

I found it interesting how that promise affected you. Later that afternoon, you were playing together in the front yard when you began arguing over whose toys belonged to whom. Amy had taken one of Aaron's trucks and he began a frustrated tirade of demands for its return. It was getting heated when suddenly Amy stopped, and in a big sister's condescending tone she said, "Aaron! Let's not get mad now, 'cause tomorrow we're going to Kona!"

All arguing immediately ceased as if some revelation or inspiration dawned new light into both of you. Aaron seemed to immediately understand, and both of you settled back into your game without a further fuss.

In a similar way, Jesus wants us to quit fussing over the petty things of this world and focus our hopes on Him. The more we focus our thoughts on our coming King, the more our present behavior will be affected. 1 John 3:3 says, "Everyone who has this hope fixed on Him purifies himself, just as He is pure."

You're going to heaven! That's the greatest hope of all — and everything else that happens here on the earth pales in comparison to that! No matter what you're going through — rejections from others, a lost job, failure to meet certain expectations — always remember: You're going to heaven! No one or nothing can take that joy away from you, for it is sealed by the work that Jesus has already accomplished on the cross!

Fix your hope on Him and His coming, and it will certainly change how you live in this present world. For when we fix our hope on Him we are purified from trivial things that really aren't important when compared to our going to heaven!

"Turn your eyes upon Jesus,

Look full in His wonderful face;

And the things of earth will grow strangely dim

In the light of His glory and grace." [1]

> Going to Kona together,
> Dad

[1] *Helen H. Lemmel, "Turn Your Eyes Upon Jesus" (Chicago: Hope Publishing Co., 1957). Copyright 1950, Renewal by H. H. Lemmel. Assigned to Alfred B. Smith.*

Happy Birthday, Jesus

Lord, help us to celebrate You
this year, and not just a holiday.

Dear Amy, Aaron, and Abby,

Wouldn't it be sad if you threw a birthday party for yourself, but when the guests arrived they began giving presents to one another instead of you? Imagine how you'd feel if no one even said, "Happy Birthday."

Try to picture it: people stroll around the room and chat about the lovely decorations and the gifts they're receiving. As all their friends arrive, they even begin to discuss how much fun it would be for them to throw a party all their own. Everyone seems to like the idea, so a couple begins to sell refreshments in one corner of the room. Some of the more artistic guests compose songs and write clever poems to be sold in a booth next to the refreshment stand. One of the partygoers asks, "What's this party about, anyway?" But no one seems to care. Everyone is enjoying themselves too much to respond.

Then, seeing how everyone is getting along quite well without you, you silently slip out the back door to watch the mirth from a distance, alone. "I thought it was my party," you ask yourself, but no one hears.

Then you feel a strong but gentle hand on your shoulder, unique only by a scar and an immediate feeling of comfort that comes with just two words — "I know," He says, "I know."

"Lord, help us to celebrate You this year, and not just a holiday. Help us to recall that as we bring our gifts unselfishly, we need not expect anything in return except the joy that comes from the invitation to Your party. Thank you that the joy of Christmas is birthed in giving — just as You were given for me."

Celebrating His birth,
Dad

Gems for
Likeness

Developing His Likeness

*When you are "born again," you
will begin to see things as Jesus
sees them, and your desires will
start to become like Jesus' desires.*

Dear Amy,

Yesterday, I went to pick you up at school.
When I walked into your classroom, one of the
first graders, Edward, said, "Are you Amy's daddy?"

"Why would you ask?" I said.

"Well, she looks just like you." Although it
doesn't seem that obvious to me, likeness is an
obvious sign of relationship. My relationship to
you showed in that likeness even before Edward
found out my name.

When we are "born again," there is a process
of likeness that begins. You will begin to see
things as Jesus sees them, and your desires will
start to become more like Jesus' desires. Don't
fight against these changes within you. John the
Baptist said, "He must increase, but I must
decrease" (John 3:30). He meant that there was
going to be more of Jesus and less of John.

In Galatians 4:19, Paul said that he wanted
Christ to be "formed" in the Galatian Christians.

That word "formed" is from the Greek word "morphos." This means a metamorphosis or a changing like a caterpillar becoming a butterfly. Inside that caterpillar is a butterfly, and a metamorphosis takes place when the "inner" becomes the "outward."

Like a tennis player who has just begun taking lessons. He watches videos of great tennis players whose "form" is exemplary. After watching and studying these tennis greats, he has that "form" in his mind, but when he attempts to duplicate that on the court, his resemblance is more like a tennis cartoon than a tennis great.

Nevertheless, he practices, disciplines himself, and under his coach's watchful care, that inner gradually becomes the outer. And little by little, he develops that tennis "form" for which the greats are known.

That is what the Bible is talking about. That Christ be "formed" in you. That the One who lives in your heart now begins to influence your words, actions, and attitudes.

My prayer, Amy is that the likeness of Jesus would be formed in you. I am praying that the inner image of Jesus in you will find outward expression in everything you do!

> Looking like Him,
> Dad

P.S. By the way, that Edward guy has an eye for good looks . . . don't you think?

Peer Pressure

*Don't let "looking right" on the
outside be your substitute for
"being right" on the inside.*

Dear Amy, Aaron, and Abby,

Each day I see people around me who spend
hundreds of dollars and hours trying to be
someone significant in their friends' eyes. They
select their clothes or cars based on popular
trends or others' opinions. Their most significant
audience is those around them. Advertisers
understand this; that's why they tell people,
"You'll make a lot of friends if you use
'toothpaste A'," or "You'll be accepted if you
drink 'cola B' just like everyone else."

We all want to be accepted, but if we are
looking to our clothes, possessions or
personality to do that, then our acceptance is
built on shaky, sandy soil. If however, our
acceptance is based on Jesus, our peace and
security will be sound because He never changes.

We live in a world that's looking good on the
outside while feeling bad on the inside. Don't let
"looking right" on the outside be your
substitute for "being right" on the inside. Let
your audience be God. Luke 2:52 says of Jesus as

He was growing up, "and Jesus kept increasing in wisdom and stature, and in favor with God and men." As you grow in favor with God first, you'll find favor with people . . . but never the other way around.

Make Jesus your audience, not your peers. You see, inevitably, we become what our audience wants us to be. Who is your audience? Let it be Jesus.

Living for an Audience of One,
Dad

True Beauty

*Ask Jesus for the kind of beauty
that comes from spending time
daily before the Lord Jesus.*

Dear Amy and Abby,

Girls your age get bombarded with lots of media images about beauty and womanhood, and many try to model themselves after those images. Most wind up disappointed and depressed because they can never measure up to the magazine models. Even if they came close, it would still be a useless attempt to fill an empty expectation. The problem is that the emphasis is all on the wrong syllable. True beauty and happiness come from what God is doing on the inside, not on how the camera makes you look on the outside. God is far more concerned with our spiritual growth and character than with outer appearances. He is less concerned with how we're looking and a whole lot more concerned with what we're becoming. But that isn't always easy. We live in a world that's looking good on the outside while feeling bad on the inside. That has become the normal course of living.

When I think of beauty I think of your mom. To me, her outer beauty increases daily. But that beauty on the outside is a reflection of the beauty Jesus has given her on the inside. I have seen and met many girls whom the world would term "attractive." Some had glamorous makeup, expensive clothes, or perfect hair, but without God's love and light in their hearts, they had no true beauty. They were merely painted, glittering shells.

One man, seeing an attractive Quaker woman, asked her for the secret of her radiant beauty. Her reply was: "For my eyes, I use compassion. For my lips, I use truth. For my hands, gentleness, and for my figure, uprightness." That's the best beauty secret I've ever heard, and that kind of beauty is far beyond "skin deep."

Ask Jesus for that gentle and quiet spirit, which the Apostle Peter says is so precious in God's sight (and mine, too). Then your beauty will be more than skin deep and it will grow daily. True beauty doesn't come by spending time every morning in front of a mirror. It comes by spending time daily before the Lord Jesus. True beauty is an inside job!

Looking to Him,
Dad

Your Image

*If you fear God, you'll fear
nothing else. If you fear man,
you'll fear everything else!*

Dear Amy and Aaron,

I've been here in Hawaii pastoring for three months now, and I love God's assignment for me. It is not because everything is going so well, but because I believe this is where God can use me most.

One thing I've especially enjoyed is playing in a church softball league. Our team has been undefeated, and recently we faced another undefeated team. We were leading 5-3 and their pitcher, who is quite competitive, started becoming abrasive. When I got up to bat, he pitched the ball before I was in the batter's box. I asked the umpire if the pitcher should wait until I got into the box, and he replied, "Yes, you can wait until you're ready, then step in." Well, the pitcher got angry and pitched another ball when I was still talking to the umpire! When I finally stepped into the box, he wouldn't throw the ball. So the umpire spoke to him, asked him to settle down, and the game continued.

I didn't think any more about it, but a week later, a friend said he had heard that I was harassing the pitcher from another team. The person spreading the rumor said it was "rude for a pastor to behave in that way." I was dumbfounded! The story, which had been turned around one-hundred-eighty degrees, was now being used to indict me.

I was disheartened for awhile until the Lord asked me, "Is what they are saying true?"

"No," I said, "those rumors are the exact opposite of what really happened!"

Then the Lord spoke to me, "Don't be involved in this. I will defend your reputation and I will be your vindicator. You take care of your heart, and I'll take care of the rest. Be secure in Me and in your right relationship with Me. Your name will not be made by the approval of men. If it is, you will always be a 'man-pleaser.' Let your reputation be made by Me. Then you'll learn to be gracious and secure, yet fearless among men."

They called Jesus a "wine-bibber," a "drunkard," a "blasphemer" and one who "frequented harlots." Do you think these assessments bothered Jesus? Do you think He stayed up all night worrying? Why not? Simply because they weren't true. Jesus was secure in who He was and He knew that the result of trying to please men before pleasing God would only be endless worry, insecurity, and compromise.

Someone once said, "If you fear God, you'll fear nothing else. If you fear man, you'll fear everything else!"

Aaron and Amy, let your reputation be formed, established, and expressed by what God is doing in you, not by what people think of you, or rather how you want people to think of you. Let God form you into His image. Otherwise, people will form you into their image. Only God can bring you the security and the freedom from trying to "protect your image." Your "image" is Jesus' likeness in you, and that doesn't need to be protected. That needs to be EXPRESSED!

Secure in His Image,
Dad

"The fear of man brings a snare, but he who trusts in the Lord will be exalted." (Proverbs 29:25)

Gems for
Obedience

Steps of Obedience

Obedience is a commitment that goes beyond what I think is comfortable.

Dear Amy, Aaron, and Abby,

Over the years, each of you has at one time or another, balked at something Mom or I have asked you to do. Usually, you wanted to know why you had to do it. But we don't always get to know why. When it comes to doing what God says, we need to obey even if we don't understand.

At the beginning of His ministry, Jesus came to John to be baptized. In Matthew's account, John was reluctant to baptize Jesus, but Jesus said to do it "to fulfill all righteousness." So John did it, even though he didn't fully understand why this was necessary.

I remember when I was in Bible College, one English professor asked us to research, "How the library came to be." This seemed about as unnecessary as learning how to repair underwear. I mean, what in the world did this have to do with becoming a "man of God" (echo and reverb needed here for effect.) It seemed so obviously unnecessary to me and a waste of many hours of study time. I procrastinated for a week or so before I went to the Lord to complain. God's reply to my heart was gracious but uncompromising:

"Did I ask you to go to Bible College?"

"Yes, Lord, but you didn't ask me to do unnecessary things!"

"Do you think I knew about this class before I sent you?"

"Well, I guess."

"Then allow it, and fulfill all righteousness."

"But Lord!"

"If I gave you a personal assignment to study about libraries, would you do it?"

"Yes, Lord."

"Then regard it as such and do it unto Me. It's part of your call to Bible College, and it is a step of obedience for you."

I then began to understand that my research was not meant to teach me about libraries as much as it was meant to teach me about obedience — joyful obedience. Obedience is a commitment that goes beyond what I think is comfortable or "good for me." God's goal was for me to learn obedience and submission through this assignment.

God is much more concerned with building our character than He is with building our knowledge. Jesus so loved and trusted the Father that He freely gave His obedience. That pleased the Father then, and that pleases the Father now.

Learning to be pleasing,
Dad

Guarding Your Heart

*Guard your heart, and don't
throw away the truth that God
has already planted in it.*

My dear Amy,

Today I was counseling a girl who really broke my heart — when I saw her heart. She had developed an appetite for the world and was in strong rebellion. She ran with the wrong crowd, and instead of being an influencer, she was the influenced. Unfortunately, she had the type of parents who controlled her entire lifestyle. It wasn't that her parents didn't love her. They just didn't know how to correctly express their love. As a result, the girl misconstrued it as being overly strict and overbearing. (I pray, Amy, that your Mom and I can correctly express our love to you without compromise.)

What really hurt was when she said, "Boy, I just wish I hadn't been raised a Christian, because I know what is right, but I don't want to do it. I like to party, drink, and hang around with whomever I want. I wished I'd never become a Christian!"

No one said that sin isn't fun when you're in the middle of it, but the consequences are deadly. It's like skydiving, and loving the sensation of weightlessness so much that you never pull your parachute chord.

What struck me was that this girl was so willing to transgress her own heart. She denied what she knew to be right and chose the wrong things anyway. By doing so, she created a lifestyle for herself based on deceptions.

Amy, Jesus has been so kind to you, giving you much truth and grace. Listen to what He is saying to you, and don't ever compromise yourself by going against your own heart. Proverbs 4:23 says, "Watch over your heart with all diligence, for from it flow the springs of life." Guard your heart, Amy, and don't throw away the truth that God has already planted in it. Invest your heart in Him alone, and He will honor that investment. If we invest our affections in the world, we will soon find that the price tag the world puts on us is far less than God's. You are priceless in God's sight and in mine!

I love you,
Dad

Recipients of the Morning Star

*"But I say to you, the rest who
are in Thyatira, who do not hold
this teaching, who have not
known the deep things of
Satan... I place no other burden
on you ... And he who overcomes
... I will give authority over the
nations... and I will give him the
Morning Star." (Rev. 2:24-29)*

My Dear Children,

In Revelation, we find a couple of phrases for
which there may not be any specific or obvious
definitions. One is "the deep things of Satan,"
and the other is "the Morning Star." Even
though these two phrases may not be easily
explainable, I do know this: the first must be just
awful and the second must be just wonderful!

Some commentators conjecture as to the
meaning of the "deep things of Satan." These
may be people whose lives have been so
deceived that they've become entrapped in
devastating habits or lifestyles which have
destroyed lives, families, and relationships. The
deep scars become lifelong battles that they have
to contend with on a daily basis. Often we hear
testimonies of notable people who have

experienced horrid backgrounds including drugs, pornography, prostitution, a life of sexual perversion, homosexuality, lesbianism, time in prison, and more. These activities have taken a toll on their lives. But somewhere along the line, by the wonderful grace of our Lord Jesus, His mercy was deeper than their deepest pit, and they came to know the Lord. These testimonies are spectacular and they are so important for us to hear again and again. Why? Because these give hope to those who may be struggling with the same lifestyles and they need to know that there is indeed a way out!

These are good testimonies!

But you want to hear the greatest testimony of all? The greatest is given by those who had the same opportunities to fall as any of the others, the same chances to involve themselves in the "deep things of Satan," but by choice, they elected not to. It is given by those who chose to serve Jesus from their youth! They may have had the same temptations but refused to give in. They put their hands to the plow and never looked back.

These have the GREATEST testimony of all!

So often people who have the greatest testimonies feel as though they have "nothing to offer." They feel as if they are "second class" Christians, and in order to have a testimony, maybe they should fall and then come back to the Lord so they can have something "spectacular" to share. That is such a deception! Instead, rejoice! You have been given the greatest testimony of all!

In the army for acts of valor, you can receive the Bronze Star or the Silver Star. Then if you had meritorious acts of valor way beyond what was expected, they give you the highest of all, a gold star that they call the Congressional Medal of Honor. These are quite prestigious!

But in God's army, those who have the greatest testimonies are given the "Morning Star."

What that is exactly, I am not sure. I do know that other stars shine only when it's dark. The Morning Star is still shining when it's light!

And moreover, it must be so prestigious to heaven that in order to describe it, the Prince of Peace Himself, the Creator of the Universe, the King of Kings, has chosen to identify with it.

"I, Jesus, have sent My angel to testify to you these things for the churches. I am the root and the offspring of David, the bright morning star." (Rev. 22:16)

Thank you for being recipients of the Morning Star!

Watching you shine,
Dad

$\mathscr{G}$ems for
Building Character

Rooted and Grounded in Love

*If you have a strong foundation
in Jesus and an attitude of
flexibility, you'll survive life's
occasional earthquakes.*

Dear Aaron, Amy, and Abby,

A couple of years ago a major earthquake hit
Hilo, and many houses were severely damaged.
Upon inspecting their homes the following morning,
owners found yawning cracks in their driveways,
roof shingles that had escaped with the wind,
and broken glass from windows that sprinkled
lawns everywhere. At that time I noticed some
things that can help us with future earthquakes.

The homes that survived the quake were
built both strong as well as flexible. Homes
made from wood withstood the earthquake
because they were able to move and sway. The
houses covered in brick or plaster were too
brittle, and they cracked with the first few tremors.

During the earthquake, everything fell to the
floors. Pots and pans were shaken from
cupboards. Fine china came crashing out of
cabinets, and valuable trinkets fell off
mantelpieces. Needless to say, many people were
deeply distraught over their losses. Interestingly,

others saw the damage as an opportunity to improve their homes. One lady in our church not only repaired her home, but also did some remodeling and additions. Now she has a beautiful room that is used for Bible studies, fellowship times, and other functions. She saw the situation not as a set-back but as an opportunity!

Sometimes things will happen in your life that will hit you as hard as an earthquake. If you have a strong foundation in Jesus and an attitude of flexibility, you'll survive life's occasional earthquakes. Even when there is damage, be quick to repair, restore, and reclaim. The final result can be something even better and more usable to the service of the King. The earthquakes aren't really the issue. They're inevitable around here. The real issue is how we handle them.

I am convinced that life is made up of 10% what happens to you and 90% how you respond to what happens to you. Life's earthquakes can make you bitter or they can make you better. The choice is up to you. Always remember this: suffering WILL change you, but not necessarily for the better. You must choose that.

Remaining flexible can only happen if you have deep roots. Then you can bend before you break. Let God build you with the right materials. Let Him add deep character to your personality and stay flexible. Earthquakes are sure to come, but the destruction that could accompany them is a negotiable option. The choice, once again, is yours.

> Choosing to be rooted in Christ,
> Dad

"That He would grant you, according to the riches of His glory, to be strengthened with power through His Spirit in the inner man; so that Christ may dwell in your hearts through faith; and that you, being rooted and grounded in love. . ." (Ephesians 3:16-17)

God's Harness

God gave you certain impulses, but
He's also given you one of the fruit
of the Spirit called "self-control."

Dear Aaron,

For a little kid, you sure ask tough questions. I can figure out hard collegiate questions, but the ones you ask often find me stumped. Questions like "Why isn't God married?" and "Why did God make dogs hate cats?" They didn't teach me how to answer those kinds of questions in Bible College.

Now you're growing as an adolescent. Your questions have a different twist to them, but still they are none the easier. You are asking questions about changes in your body and questions about girls. (By the way, your mom would love to answer these kinds of questions. I'll stick to the ones about God.)

The other week, I was with some college students, and one asked ... no, challenged me with this question, "If God didn't intend for us to be sexually active, then why did He give us these urges and appetites for sex? Obviously they are for us to engage in!"

You can tell a lot about people by the questions they ask. You can tell a lot about their hearts by the spirit in which the question is asked.

You'll wonder too about the impulses that are surfacing. Your hormones will begin to boil when you're around certain girls, and you will feel certain urges that you've not felt before. So, what should you do? Go headlong in following after these?

When I was in high school, I used to run sprints. One day, my coach strapped a vest onto me with a rope attached to the back of it. It was sort of like a harness, and it ran through a pulley. He could then control the speed of my sprinting by adjusting the tension on the pulley.

I remember in practice, he'd fire the starting gun, and off I'd go. Cinders would be flying, my muscles straining, but with this harness on, I'd be "flying" at about five miles per hour.

After twenty-five yards or so, he'd "reel" me back in, adjust my form, and I'd repeat this whole ordeal. His reasoning behind the harness was that to be a great sprinter, I would need to develop certain muscles called "twitch" muscles. By controlling my speed and adding resistance when I ran, these muscles would be strengthened. Then, when he took the harness off, I rocketed out of the blocks! And over the hundred meters or so, my muscles would be well conditioned to stay strong and vibrant till the end.

Sometimes, God puts a harness on your desires and impulses. Although the hormones are there, it doesn't mean that your character muscles are developed enough to take you to the end. This is why so many relationships breakdown at the midway point. They cramp up or simply give out.

God gave you certain impulses, but He's also given you one of the fruit of the Spirit called "self-control." Let God develop the right muscles of character and discipline. Don't throw off the harness. Too many have, and the devastating results are everywhere. Then one day, after doing it God's way, He will bring you the right person to marry. Then when you come out of the blocks, it will be a rocket-blast! And you'll stay strong till the very end, and the joy of doing it God's way will be so rewarding!

And one day when looking through the rearview mirror of life, you will see how wonderful God has been to you and your family. Then you'll ask, "Why doesn't everyone do it God's way?!" And I will still be unable to answer your questions.

In training,
Dad

The Setting of a Gem

*Then when God sees that the
setting is ready, He will be
faithful to place His very best
gems in your life! That's when
you'll shine!*

Dear Amy, Aaron, and Abby,

I saw a lady's five-carat diamond ring the
other day. Wow! Was that ever impressive! That
diamond must have been worth $30,000! The
band was a simple gold band with a few smaller
diamonds on either side. Holding the diamond
in place was a setting that included maybe five or
six "fingers."

"My!" I thought. "That setting had better be
strong! It's holding onto $30,000!"

Although the setting doesn't get as much
attention as the diamond itself, it is equally
important. Any wise jeweler would never put
such a precious jewel in a poor or weak setting!
If he did, then one small bump and the gem
would be lost! The strength and quality of the
setting will determine the security and staying
power of the gem!

Character is like that setting. God has promised us such wonderful gems! Yet without the basis of character, these gems, His promises, would be lost or forfeited at the first bump we hit!

> *"Eye has not seen and ear has not heard, and which have not entered the heart of man, all that God has prepared for those who love Him."* (1 Corinthians 2:9)

The Holy Spirit's desire is to produce character in each of us prior to the setting of the gems. Whether those gems are marriage, an influential position, a ministry, finances, or a family, each of these will require character. This is the setting that needs to be developed prior to the placement of the gem.

Galatians 5:22 gives us some of the character qualities God wants to produce in us. They are called the "fruit of the Spirit;" Love, joy, peace, patience, kindness, goodness, faithfulness, gentleness, and self-control. Every single one of these is necessary to the promise! When we get impatient about God's promises coming to pass, we must always remember that we're not waiting on God. He's waiting on us! And like a wise jeweler, God doesn't want to put a precious gem in a faulty setting!

Strengthen your setting. That's your responsibility. Build your character. Learn to forgive, to be diligent, to be honest. Learn to stay steady and faithful, to keep commitments, to go by what you know and not necessarily by what you feel.

Here's a simple definition of character that I heard along the way . . .

"Character is the ability to follow through on a worthy commitment long after the emotion of making that commitment has passed."

God will refine your metal till it's pure gold. He will shape your character till it's strong and trustworthy. Then when God sees that the setting is ready, He will be faithful to place His very best gems in your life! That's when you'll shine!

"Let your light shine before men in such a way that they may see your good works and glorify your Father who is in heaven." (Matthew 5:16)

Love,
Dad

Sometimes, God Leaves Us Alone

*Sometimes God will let you struggle
and there will be none to help.*

Dear Amy,

Sometime ago, when our church office was in an old home in Hilo, I learned a painful, but never-to-be-forgotten lesson!

The windows were old and seldom used since we had air conditioning. One Saturday, I decided to clean the office. Not wanting to bother anyone else, I went down there alone and figured it would be a nice way to spend the afternoon.

My first task was to clean the windows. Now these windows were of the archaic and obsolete style. They slid up and down in two parts with ropes attached to weights to offset each window. These ropes and weights were hidden in the walls. The upper half and bottom half were heavy, old wooden windows that slid adjacent to each other.

Anyway, I opened the bottom one by grabbing the top of it and pulling upwards. While I had my hands grasping the window, the top window came sliding down, wedging my fingers between them. The pain was excruciating. It was like slamming a car door on your fingers, but because both hands were caught, I had no way of opening it!

It felt like my fingers were broken. I called for help, but there was no one to help! I was all alone. Every emotion imaginable surged through my body. I was scared, and then angry because no one was there to help. Then I felt abandoned, ashamed. I wondered how long I'd be trapped there with my fingers wedged between the windows. Maybe they'd realized something was wrong when I didn't show up for dinner or for church on Sunday. At least they'd find me by Monday!

I started to cry because it hurt so badly. Then I gave up trying, and I began praying. I thought maybe God could help. I pleaded with the Lord and just then, I got an idea!

Using my foot as leverage, I dislodged the stuck window using my teeth just enough to pry my fingers loose! I was free at last! My fingers resembled a bunch of smashed pipe cleaners. They were a bit bloody, but not broken!

You know, Amy, sometimes God is the last one we go to for help instead of the first. We look to others for encouragement, assistance, acceptance, and companionship. We do that until we're almost addicted! When that happens, God is forgotten!

I remember the first time you quoted John 3:16. You said, "For God so loved the world that He sent His only forgotten Son..." I think about that and chuckle, but at the same time I think, "How true!"

Psalm 107:12 says this: "They stumbled and there was none to help. Then they cried out to the Lord in their trouble; and He saved them out of their distress."

Sometimes God will let you struggle and there will be none to help. When that happens, don't get mad at people. Don't play the blame game. Instead, cry out to the Lord. Maybe God removed the people to return your heart back home to Him! Cry out to the Lord at the beginning of the pinch, not when you're about to faint from the pain.

God is the Source of your help. When there's no one around, He will always be there for you. Reach out your hands, before they get pinched, and they won't resemble a bunch of smashed pipe cleaners.

Hand-in-hand,
Dad

Gems for
Guidance and Discipline

Good News!

*Because we want God's best, we must
quickly cooperate with His commands.*

My dear son Aaron,

Let me give you a quick lesson in Greek. The Greek word "Euangelion" that we translate as gospel really means "good news". However, sometimes people say, "Oh, the Bible is just filled with a bunch of do's and don'ts. That's not good news to me!"

It's true that the Bible contains many do's and don'ts. But often, people can't see the value of these guidelines because they are looking at them through windows of selfishness or unbelief. It's no wonder they perceive Jesus as "religion" rather than as a friend and shepherd.

The Bible's do's and don'ts are directions from the Good Shepherd saying, "Go through this door . . . oops not through that one . . . oh yes, through this one, for it will lead to the fullness of the Father's design for you. No, don't go through that door for it leads to a dead end."

One day, I received a wonderful anonymous gift — my choice of an expensive new suit. After browsing the store for some time, I finally selected one and put it on so the tailor could alter it to my size. He put his measuring tape around his neck, put his pins in his mouth and started measuring, "Stand up straight, please. Turn left, legs together. Turn right. Arms up, now down." I wanted him to give me the best fit possible, so when he asked me to turn left, I didn't say, "Forget it! Don't tell me what to do!" Rather, I wanted to do exactly as he said. Why? Because I wanted the suit to be tailored correctly so it would fit! What do you think the suit would have looked like in the end if I refused to cooperate with his directions? What do you think I would have looked like wearing that suit!

So it is with Jesus, Aaron. He's the Master Tailor, fitting us into His kingdom. Because we know He wants only what's best for us, we can quickly and confidently obey His commands. Cooperate with His directives! Don't question Him. He's knows exactly what He is doing, and the sooner we obey, the better we look! Now that's "good news!"

> With much love,
> Your Dad

Sensitive Responses

*Being sensitive to God means
responding daily to the little
things He tells you.*

Dear Amy,

Right now I'm at the Honolulu airport, waiting for a flight to Hilo. It's crowded with people, rushing excitedly here and there. Some are vacationing and still others are on important business trips. They're all so different, yet I see in each a heart that Jesus wants to touch. I wonder how many of them are concerned about their eternities. Are they so caught up in their own little worlds that they cannot feel Jesus reaching out to touch them?

Most of them are busy with the tasks at hand. They seem happy enough, but are they really? I have to wonder if they, like many of us, simply choose to fill life with shallow substitutes for God's reality. I think we sometimes keep ourselves busy so as to ignore the pain in our lives. It's kind of like taking codeine. It numbs our pain, but cannot heal our wounds. It may even make our injuries worse because we may continue to use our hurt limbs instead of seeking treatment.

You know, Amy, sometimes Jesus will touch a place in your life and it will pain you a bit. You will sense some hurt and feel uncomfortable. But instead of trying to ignore that feeling, respond to it. It will be the Holy Spirit tugging on your heart. We tend to pump our souls with anesthetic to numb the spirit and deaden the pain, then we wonder why we can't hear God anymore. Being sensitive to God means responding daily to the little things He tells you. The more we respond, making daily adjustments in our hearts and actions, the more sensitive we become to God's voice inside.

"Lord Jesus, so many times people will tell us to be tough and unaffected. Lord, help me to be vulnerable instead. I don't want to be numb to You — so caught up in this world that it deadens me to Your voice or Your plans. Keep Amy and I sensitive to You and Your Spirit daily. Amen."

In the love of Him who wept over Jerusalem,
Dad

Embracing Boundaries

*May God help us to see that the
boundaries around our lives are
not walls of concrete or banks of
dirt, but hands of His love.*

My dear son Aaron,

I just read about a huge flood in Colorado.
One of the area's dams gave way, and an
overpowering wall of water destroyed property
and injured people. In its rightful place, the
water was very useful — for needed irrigation,
crops, and perhaps, after filtering, for drinking.
But outside of its boundaries, that useful water
turned into a destructive force which resulted in
much ruin and hurt.

Aaron, Jesus has given you energy, zeal, and
boldness in certain areas, and to harness those
qualities into something useful, God has placed
boundaries around you. These boundaries are
not designed to hinder nor frustrate you, but
rather to protect your potential! Without
boundaries, a beautiful lake would be nothing
but a swamp, only good for breeding
mosquitoes and snakes. Without boundaries,
the water would try to go everywhere at the same
time without direction and purpose.

Aaron, sometimes you won't understand why these boundaries are placed around you, and you'll have a tendency to push against them. But instead, be thankful for them.

May God help us to see that the boundaries around our lives are not walls of concrete or banks of dirt, but hands of His love; huge hands that embrace our lives, hands that we can rest in. God knows exactly what's best, and even if your boundaries are beyond your understanding, they will never be beyond your faith.

In His embrace,
Dad

Don't Cross the Line

*God is a loving Father and He
knows the future . . . He simply
says, "Thou shall not." Then the
rest of the Bible tells us why not.*

Dear Abby,

You turned three years old this week. Let me
tell you a bit about your mom. She seems to be
a "frustrated spray-paint artist." She painted a
foursquare game on our driveway "just for fun,"
and then the other day, she added a line at the
end of the driveway that you're not supposed to
cross with your tricycle. (When friends are
looking for our house now, they just look for
the graffiti driveway!)

Mom took you over to the line and said,
"Don't cross this line!" You, at the age of three,
could understand! She could have explained it
first by saying, "If you transgress this line to
enter the street, you'll enter a dangerous
parameter where your chance of being hurt rises
64.5%. You will increase your chances to be
impacted by an automotive projectile traveling at
30 miles per hour. Your small stature combined
with the automobile's inertia of motion, will
result in multiple lacerations and sub-dural

hematomas requiring extensive surgery and suturing." At this point, I think you'd be clueless to what she was trying to say.

Sometimes when Mom or Dad says "NO," you may not understand. You'll get upset and want to "cross the line" anyway because you can't see anything wrong. It's at these times you need to realize that the "NO" comes from a Mom and Dad who love you dearly. One day, you'll look back and understand, but until then, God has given you parents through which He speaks.

Lately, we've been studying the Ten Commandments and I've come to appreciate them more and more. I've been understanding the "whys" behind each command, and that God wrote them for my benefit, not His convenience. Each one comes from the heart of a loving Father, not from the fist of an insecure dictator. The way I respond to each of the commandments says a lot about my maturity. If I cannot respond to these ten, I can't move on to greater privileges, responsibilities, and trust levels.

God is a loving Father and He knows the future. He also knows our capacity to understand, so He simply says, "Thou shall not." Then the rest of the Bible tells us why.

One day you'll learn about sub-dural hematomas, but you'll want to learn about them from books, not from an experience of disobedience.

Lining up with God's best,
Dad

Grace and Liberty

The more we know about God's laws, the more at liberty we are and the more fulfilled we'll be!

My dear Amy,

Whenever I write to you, I'm always thinking about how much I love you. I hope that always comes through in my letters. I was thinking today how much I appreciate my heavenly Father's many expressions of love to me in the Bible. This wonderful book is His eternal love letter to us. Isaiah 40:8 says, "The grass withers, the flower fades, but the word of our God stands forever."

Even His commandments are expressions of His love! Many times we may think His commands bind us, but please don't ever let Satan deceive you that way. The more we know about God's laws, the more liberty we have and the more fulfilled we'll be!

The other day I was driving in my car and I stopped at a red light behind someone. Now if you are turning right onto a one-way street here in Hawaii, the law permits you to do so even though the light is red. Unless there's a sign specifically prohibiting that, you may proceed after stopping.

Well, this person obviously didn't know about the law. Although the car's right-turn signal was on and there were no cars coming, she just sat there. There were other cars behind me with right-turn signals flashing, but we all had to wait because this person obviously wasn't aware of the law. I don't like it when people honk their horns at me, so I don't beep at others. Instead, I talk to them from inside my car. No, I don't yell. I just coach. And on this occasion, I found myself "coaching" her enthusiastically from my driver's seat.

"Lady, don't you know you can go? Read your manual please! Beep! Lady, beep!" But all my verbal honking was to no avail. The signal finally changed, and we all began moving.

"Whew, Lord," I thought to myself, "if that lady only knew the law better, we wouldn't have had to sit there and wait!" It was then that the Lord spoke to my heart and said, "The same thing applies to My Laws, Wayne. The more you know it, the more freedom you'll have. I didn't write my laws to bind you, but to give you an increased liberty! Know my Word, and the Truth it contains, for . . .

"You shall know the truth, and the truth shall make you free." (John 8:32)

Making right turns,
Dad

Gems for
Changing Your Perspective

Attitudes

*One of the most important
decisions you'll ever make in life
is the attitude with which you
will serve Him.*

Dear Abby, Aaron and Amy,

Attitudes are often more important than
facts. Your attitude today is more important
than your appearance, education, skills, money,
or past. I am more and more convinced that life
is only 10% circumstances. The other 90% is how
you respond to those circumstances.

Your attitude will make you or break you,
make you a friend or a foe, bring joy to a
situation or sorrow. You may not have control
over what others do or how people treat you,
but you do have full control over how you
respond to the way they treat you. God has
given each of us full control over our attitude.
No one can take that away. You, and you alone,
are responsible for that.

The most important decision you'll make in
life is your decision to follow Jesus. I am so glad
you've made that decision. Let me tell you about
your second most important decision: the
attitude with which you will follow the Lord.

In Matthew 5, the first teaching Jesus formally gives His disciples has nothing to do with ministry skills, how to battle the Pharisees, or how to become famous or successful. Instead, He teaches them how to have good attitudes! This is why we call the first seminar Jesus held for His disciples the "Be-attitudes," because your attitudes will determine what you will "be." (This is from my own commentary on Matthew...)

I am convinced that Jesus is less concerned with what we are doing and a whole lot more concerned with what we are becoming! That has a lot to do with my attitude.

You are the sum total of all your attitudes. Check your heart and even if you don't do all things perfectly, you can still do them with a smile!

Straight from the heart,
Dad

Prescription for Boredom

*Don't let boredom bar you from
some of God's very best. Renew
your mind and get involved!*

My dear Amy,

The other day, I stopped by the local elementary school before classes began. I was talking with the teacher overseeing the kindergarten class. Although school hadn't started yet, she was rounding up the kids into the room. One little boy however, was quite contrary and kept going outside.

Finally the teacher dragged him into the room by his backpack and demanded, "Now stay in this room until the bell rings!"

"Boring!" he replied in a monotone voice.

"I don't care," said the teacher, "you get in and stay here!"

"Boooring," he said slowly, trying to make the word sound exactly like its definition.

I just had to laugh as I watched this tiny kid with a red backpack, an angry, frustrated teacher, and one monotone word between them,

"Boooring."

She finally took his backpack off and ushered him into a crowd of other kids. She did her best to involve him in some games and an art project with colorful paints. He seemed slow to engage, but when I peeked into the classroom a few minutes later, he was having a great time playing! It wasn't boring after all! His boredom did not come from the classroom. It came from his unwillingness to be involved!

In general, boredom comes from a lack of involvement. If you think a class is boring, try participating more. Raise your hand and say what you think or volunteer for games. I'll bet your boredom with that class will disappear.

Church is the same way. If it seems uninteresting, I'd check out my participation before I'd check out from church. Sometimes, relationships can also grow dull. When that happens, I try to invest myself more. When I counsel couples who say their marriage is boring, I tell them to become more involved in each other's lives.

Don't let boredom bar you from God's very best. Say "yes" more than you say "no." Take off the backpack of wrong attitudes, renew your mind and get involved! Life's great!

Jumping into life,
Dad

A Privileged Perspective

*God will often give you a certain
perspective into situations, not in
order to see what's wrong, but in
order to support, help, and serve
more effectively.*

Dear Aaron,

At one of your baseball games this season,
they needed a scorekeeper. Although I wasn't
excited to volunteer, I went up on the balcony
overlooking home plate and kept score. Your
team had been badly losing every game, and the
coach had asked the parents for their help. Each
game, however, was so embarrassing, I wasn't sure
if I really wanted to identify myself as a parent.

From the score box, I noticed that the
elevated vantage point gave me the best seat in
the house! The game began, and with classic
form, your team began to reel under the
destructive force of your opponent. (The final
score was 36 to 7.) But from that view above the
backstop, I could clearly see every player's errors
and blunders. Even the coach and assistant made
horrendous miscalculations. They substituted
players incorrectly causing total bedlam. They
put wrong players in the wrong positions, and
he had you bunt when you should have swung

away. I made a list of all the foibles so I could present them to the coach after the game. (After all, he asked for help from the parents, didn't he?)

Last inning, and the punishment from the other team was finally over. I grabbed my list and was ready to share my "expertise" with the coaches, but the Lord stopped me. For some reason, He wouldn't let any criticism come out of my mouth! Instead, I found myself encouraging the coaches much like Balaam did when he was paid to curse Israel but could only bless them instead! The list was never mentioned. For some reason, I felt strongly that God was not allowing me to share my "expertise" and wonderful knowledge.

Later at home I prayed, "Lord, I know exactly what they did wrong. I was the most qualified to tell them because I saw it all from the scorekeeper's box. I had the best view!"

Then the Lord said, "I don't give you a privileged perspective so you can curse people. I give you this perspective so you'll know how to support, help, and serve them more effectively. You will see where they are weak, but don't abuse this perspective. It is not to magnify their weakness. It is not for ammunition against them. Instead now you can pray more accurately! Don't curse foolishly! If you cannot use this privileged perspective I give you, then you will no longer have that vantage point. Be faithful with it. It is a gift that I am entrusting to you with which to serve My people."

Aaron, sometimes the Lord will let us see people from a different viewpoint. You'll see their faults and weaknesses. Can God trust you with that view? Will you use your vantage point to support people or abuse it and condemn them? Gossip, grumbling, complaining, and condemning are all abuses of God's viewpoint.

God knows enough about you and me to sink both our ships, yet He loves and supports us instead. Can He trust you to do the same with what you see? When you can be trusted with His eyes, He'll entrust you with His heart.

Seeing things His way,
Dad

God Vindicates the Righteous

*Wait on the Lord. He will
rearrange your view of things.*

Dear Aaron, Abby, and Amy,

Yesterday ranks as one of the worst days I've
ever experienced as a pastor. A lady came in for a
supposed "counseling" session. As soon as she
sat down, she began to unload her guns on me
and proceeded to accuse me of taking God's
money for my own use, using poor judgement,
for bad preaching and for being a poor leader.
For one solid hour she berated me, the church,
the Sunday School, and the leadership. She even
made an especially bold accusation about your
mom. I usually don't get riled up, but when she
started attacking your mom, I was ready to
rearrange her face! This lady had heard a second-
hand story about your mom, and she took it as
"gospel truth." (I often wonder why people
receive the Gospel as optional and gossip as fact.)

I wanted to clear up the situation, so I asked
her if I could call the other person involved right
then and there during the counseling session. I
felt that if I could get the story from the one
who concocted it, we could take care of this
whole thing and save me from having to sit
through rumors she was taking as fact. She

vehemently replied, "No," and because of that, I tabled the rest of the "counseling session" till we got more facts. I asked her to speak with the other person again to ensure the story was accurate.

That night I went home broken, discouraged, and ready to resign. All of her accusations were way off base. I was doing the very best I knew how to serve God's people, and I had let this missile find its mark, and I was hurting. Proverbs says that God will vindicate the righteous, and I believe that. I just have a difficult time waiting for Him to make His final ruling!

Later that evening, God showed me His grace. The third person involved called and apologized, and the lady (the one who needed her face remodeled?) called me and asked my forgiveness for her wrong conclusions. Of course I forgave her. How glad I was that everything was cleared up! I learned so much that day especially about trusting God to repair things that I couldn't!

When you are falsely accused and want to rearrange someone's face, wait on the Lord. He rearranges their hearts as well as your view of things. His way is a whole lot better (and a lot less messy).

Trusting in Him,
Dad

Gems for
Forgiveness

Stolen Blessings

*God wants an unbroken
friendship with us so He can give
us the fullness of His blessings.*

My dear son Aaron,

You are eleven years old. Yesterday I wanted to take you golfing with me after work. I know how much you like to drive the golf cart, and I was so excited to give you this outing as a "gift." I was really looking forward to spending some time with you. I love watching the excitement in your eyes as you navigate the sand traps and the sprinkler heads in your imagined "Army Jeep." All day I was thinking about our outing together. I simply told you that I had a "gift" and that I would give it to you after school. You were so excited as you went off to catch the morning bus.

But when I got home, I found Mom very upset with you. She said you had disobeyed her and caused her a lot of grief by stealing a small item at the grocery store. She announced to me that you were grounded and had to stay in your room the rest of the afternoon.

When I heard that, my heart was broken. Not only because you had disobeyed, but because I could not give you my "gift." Rather than going out for a round of golf, you were restricted to your room as a consequence of your disobedience. I was saddened because that incident stole our time together.

When we sin, God feels that way, too. Luke 12:32 says, "...your Father has chosen gladly to give you the kingdom." He desires to bless you. God says in Jeremiah 5:25, "... your sins have withheld good from you." He wants to give us so much, but our sin forfeits His blessings. God's heart is broken by our sin because it breaks our fellowship with Him — like the fellowship you and I could have enjoyed on the golf course.

Obeying the Lord isn't a burdensome thing when you look at it with God's eyes. He wants an unbroken friendship with us so He can give us the fullness of His blessings.

I hope we can go golfing soon. You can even drive the cart.

Because of love,
Dad

No Condemnation

*God's gift of forgiveness always
comes with another gift. It's
called wisdom. Take them both.
They come two to a package.*

Dear Amy, Abby, and Aaron,

We all fail at various times, but for many
people these failures become huge burdens that
keep them from moving forward in the future. I
love the Good News of Jesus Christ because it
constantly reminds me of a God who never
condemns us to our past, but instead redeems
us from it!

There will come a time when you will fail
miserably — you'll fail in what you know to be
right, you'll reject what Dad and Mom told you,
and you may even turn your back on Jesus. The
pain you'll feel then will weigh you down, and
Satan will be quick to lay his condemnation on
you. But don't accept it! Instead embrace God's
forgiveness. When you fail, never let the devil
deal with your failure. Let God! Confess your
sin. Don't tuck it away because it will not get
resolved by ignoring it. Always remember that it
is not necessarily sin that kills God's people. It's
unresolved sin.

"When I kept silent about my sin, my body wasted away, through my groaning all day long. For day and night Thy hand was heavy upon me; My vitality was drained away as with the fever heat of summer." (Ps. 32:3,4)

You can see a picture here about sin's devastating effects on our lives and even on our physical bodies! Someone once said, "Every time I hide my sin, my stomach keeps score."

But take a look at the beauty of confessing and revealing our sin to the Lord: "I acknowledged my sin to Thee, and my iniquity I did not hide; I said, 'I will confess my transgressions to the Lord.' and Thou didst forgive the guilt of my sin." (Ps. 32:5)

A person once came to me and said, "Isn't it true that people who were right will end up in heaven, and the people that were wrong will end up in hell?" My answer to him was, "Not exactly. The Bible says we all have sinned, so we were all wrong! But the ones who will end up in heaven will be the people who were wrong, but admitted it. The ones who will end up in hell are the ones who were likewise wrong, but refused to admit it."

When I remember my frailties, faults, and problems, they keep me humble. It is a constant reminder of the grace of God. If it weren't for His grace, I would be in terrible shape! But He keeps lifting me up and He helps me to focus on the future. When I begin to think that God will never be able to use me, I think of the failures of great men and women of God, and I take courage:

With Moses, it was murder.

With Elijah, it was deep depression.

With Peter, it was public denial.

With Samson, it was recurring lust.

With Thomas, it was cynical doubting.

With Jacob, it was deception.

With Rahab, it was prostitution.

"If Thou, Lord shouldst mark our iniquities, O Lord, who could stand? But there is forgiveness with Thee...." (Ps. 130:3) If God were to keep score, we'd all be done for! Seek His mercy and His grace. Respect these gifts when you receive them and when God gives you His forgiveness, there will always be another gift that comes along with it. It is called wisdom. Wisdom comes so you won't repeat the error. Receive them both. These gifts come two to a package. Never take only forgiveness and not be wiser because of it!

God is so much greater than our failures. Don't ever let them condemn you. Let God's grace lift you above them and give you a new start! His mercies are new every morning! Ask for His forgiveness, renew your commitment to Him above all else, and then go to sleep! The morning starts another day of being forgiven . . .

And being loved,
Dad

Second Chances

All God wants are teachable hearts, unsatisfied with being C-average Christians.

Dear Amy,

Yesterday, I got a painful lesson in the difference between acceptable behavior and wise behavior. Acceptable behavior is simply doing what is expected of you, kind of like doing "C" work. You don't make waves and don't offend anyone. Unfortunately, nothing significant happens either. You go through your day without bringing any zest, impact, or flavor to anyone's life!

My "C" day started when I was getting my driver's license renewed at the police station. While I was there, the mayor walked in and started talking to people. I felt prompted to go over, introduce myself, and tell him that I was going to pray for him and his leadership. But I didn't follow through. I was too shy, and actually, I didn't want to do anything "out of the ordinary." So I didn't bother him. I also didn't give God a chance to do anything significant in his life either.

Later on, I bought some poinsettias for a lady in our church who was sick, and when I was walking back to my car, I passed a tavern. A barmaid was standing just outside the door, crying. I felt prompted to give her the flowers and tell her that Jesus knew about her tears. Again I passed the opportunity by. I didn't want to do anything out of the ordinary. I was satisfied with acceptable behavior, and as a result, I didn't make a difference in that woman's life.

Driving down the road, there was a man held a cardboard sign asking for work. He looked willing and genuine. I guess he had just hit on some hard times and even a couple hours of work might help him to get some dinner for his family. The car in front of me stopped next to the man, rolled his window down, made a rude comment, cursed and drove off. I saw the face and heart of the willing worker drop. He awkwardly glanced at the ground embarrassed, and didn't even look up when I drove by. Although I was angry at the insensitive driver, I didn't do much better. I simply drove on by like the righteous Levite passing the wounded traveler on the way to Jericho. I didn't want to do anything out of the ordinary.

Afterwards, I felt so inadequate. I asked Jesus to give me another chance, and He has. In fact, today, I've already had several new opportunities to encourage people! God is so good. He never speaks to us with words of condemnation, but rather in words of invitation ... yes, an invitation to another chance! And He will give you another chance, too. Watch for it. Don't ever settle for "acceptable" Christian behavior. All He wants are teachable hearts, people who are wise enough to be unsatisfied with being C-average Christians.

I'm so glad Jesus didn't settle for an average life! I'm so glad He reached out to me and did something "out of the ordinary"! And He will give you the chance to take that baton and continue living life above the average! Take it.

Because of a second chance,
Dad

*G*ems for
Refinement

Revealing Your Heart

*As God develops your heart, your
words will be gracious and kind.*

Dear Abby,

I had quite a surprise at the airport this
morning. While waiting with a friend for our
flight to depart, we noticed some passengers
getting on another plane. Among them was a
pretty young woman (about eighteen or so),
who looked like she was returning home from a
vacation. Their arms were packed with souvenirs
and memorabilia. She and her mother arrived
late and were obviously anxious to get on board.

Unfortunately, the flight was overbooked
and they (along with several others) got
bumped. They were told that they would have to
wait another two hours for the next flight. One
girl started crying. Others moaned and complained.
I felt sorry for them hoping that the airline could
find an optional route for their return.

I went back to the book I was reading and a
few minutes later, my attention was captured by
an escalating conversation that abruptly broke
into shouting and cursing. The anger was
directed at one of the airline agents behind the
customer service counter. Although the attendant

was doing her best to stay calm, she reminded me of a wooden shed in a hurricane just before being swept away. (Those people just don't get paid enough for what they have to endure!)

They were using such terrible language, I turned to see what was happening. When I looked behind me, the person leading the "charge" was the young woman I described earlier. She was swearing like an old sailor, using quite descriptive words and creative phrases, ones that I hadn't even thought of ... even in my "B.C." days! Her heart was quickly revealed in a time of tension. Her mouth made it known.

Someone once said that tension doesn't develop character. It only reveals it. Ouch.

"For the mouth speaks out of that which fills the heart." Matthew 12:34

We will always reveal the contents of our hearts, good or bad, through our words. That's why it's important to ask God for a pure heart, honey. As God develops your heart, your words will become gracious and kind. God is making you into a beautiful girl, and that beauty doesn't begin with your face and hair. It begins with your heart.

Going back to the Source,
Dad

Repairing Your Zeal

*Let Jesus heal your motivation
and spirit, and He will make you
even stronger.*

Dear Aaron,

You recently received your first bicycle —
training wheels and all. You rode it up and down
the driveway on Christmas morning, in the rain
and without shoes! You rode it again yesterday,
and I warned Mom to get ready to bandage your
knees.

Sure enough, you came racing down the
driveway, turned too quickly, and down you
went. Your mother covered her eyes in terror as
you scraped your face and tore your bike seat.
I've never understood why she does that.
Afterward she patiently fixed you up and dried
your tears. She listened to your complaints with
encouraging words and extra hugs.

Even though you took a bad spill, you were
ready to go again the next day. You were
determined to ride your bicycle and conquer the
mystery of balance. Soon, I will be taking those
training wheels off, and you'll be jumping ramps
and curbs. Your next bike may even end up with
a 250 cc engine attached to it. (And Mom will be
covering her eyes again!)

Sometimes, son, when there's a "spill" in your life, the pain and the tears will delay you, but they can't defeat you. Your biggest enemy won't be a scraped elbow or face; it will be a scraped motivation. It won't be a torn seat that will stop you; it will be torn zeal.

Get up and go for it again, Aaron. When you do that, you'll succeed. I'm sure of it! Let Jesus heal your motivation and spirit, and He will make you even stronger. You will serve Him and do well. (And this time your mom won't have to cover her eyes.)

Being righteous in God's eyes does not mean you won't fall. Being righteous means you are willing to get up and try again! "The righteous falls seven times, but rises again!" (Proverbs 24:16) What matters more than how high you've blown up is what direction your feet are pointing when you touch ground again!

Let me share a poem with you. I got it from the Reader's Digest. It's an anonymous poem, but the truth of it makes it downright personal. Here it is. It's called "Anyway."

People are unreasonable, illogical, self-centered. Love them ... ANYWAY.

If you do good, people will accuse you of selfish, ulterior motives. Do good ... ANYWAY.

If you are successful, you'll win false friends and true enemies. Succeed ... ANYWAY.

Honesty and frankness may make you vulnerable. Be honest and frank ... ANYWAY.

The good you do today may be forgotten tomorrow. Do good ... ANYWAY.

The biggest people with the biggest ideas can be shot down by the smallest people with the smallest minds. Think big ... ANYWAY.

Give the world the best you've got. You may very well get kicked in the teeth for it. But give the world the best you've got ... ANYWAY!

Serving Jesus joyfully . . . Anyway!
Dad

Walking In Integrity

*By taking small steps to keep our
word, we have a deeper
understanding of how God
always keeps His Word.*

Dear Aaron,

There's a saying that goes, "I can't hear what
you say, because what you do speaks so loudly!"
Our lifestyle and actions build a platform upon
which we speak, and that will either support or
nullify what we say. Our lifestyle will either add
to or take away the credibility of our words. In
the old days, a man's word was as good as a
signed contract. Although the standards for
integrity have slipped in our contemporary
culture, a Christian's word should still be as
trustworthy as a contract! Being men who walk
in integrity is very important to our faith.

We catch a glimpse of God's integrity as we
try to be trustworthy. By taking small steps to
keep our word, we have a deeper understanding
of how God always keeps His Word. As our trust
in God grows, so will our obedience to Him.

A few summers ago, I was learning to rappel
in Montana on the side of a 300 foot cliff. The
instructor was very good, but his assistant
seemed a bit green. When he strapped me into

my harness, the main instructor had to come over and redo it. That was the only warning I needed to alert me that this guy was not "expert" enough. We split up into two lines, and I was put in the assistant's group. I peeked over the edge and my life flashed before my eyes. We neared the edge of the cliff, and when the assistant gave me instructions, I doubted his expertise and hesitated. Here I was, a man with dreams for his future, and I was supposed to suspend all those dreams by a 1/2 inch rope completely in the hands of a greenhorn? I thought to myself, "Get real! There's no way I'm that much of an idiot!"

When he asked me to tie the rope on and lean out over the cliff, I told him I needed to use the bathroom first, and disappeared. A few minutes later, I returned and instead of going back to my line, I weaseled my way into the main instructor's group. I told him I was a late enrollment who loved life.

Finally the moment came when he checked my harness and coached me toward the edge. Though my heart was still thumping, I was more willing to obey him because I trusted him.

Do you trust God? Do you have faith in His instruction? Do you believe that His advice is good and that He will keep His word?

A great way to build your trust in God is to begin with yourself. Do you keep your word? If you say you're going to empty the trash, do you do it? If you say you're going to meet someone for lunch, are you there on time?

Mark 11 holds the classic teaching of "mountain-moving faith."

> *"Truly I say to you, whosoever says to this mountain, 'Be taken up and cast into the sea' and does not doubt in his heart, but believes that what he says is going to happen, it shall be granted him." (Mark 11:23)*

I observed an intriguing lesson about faith. Notice it says that if I say to the mountain, "Be removed and cast into the sea" and I don't doubt in my heart and I believe what I say will come to pass, it will be done.

Here are two irreducible qualities of faith.

First, it is my responsibility to deal with the doubts in my heart. If there are any doubts at all about what I am planning to do, it is my responsibility to resolve them before I move on. Whether it is through prayer, research, fasting, or counsel, I must resolve any lingering doubts prior to my launching out in faith. Whether it is a marriage, an investment, relationship, or job change, don't move ahead till you've worked out the doubts!

The second irreducible quality is this. God says that I must believe what I say if I'm going to believe what God says! If I am not holding myself accountable to integrity, then my trust-factor in God's Word will be inadequate for His assignments for me.

Building faith in your own words is important because it helps you to build faith in God's Word. Learn to "walk in your integrity." A person with character richness, who walks in his integrity, is of great value in God's eyes. And like that rappelling instructor, if people can trust you, they'll weasel a way to get into your group more often than any other.

Leaning on Jesus,
Dad

Pruning Pains

*If I want to be a "fruit-bearing"
tree in the Kingdom, I'd better
plan on getting pruned.*

Dear Aaron,

I have been pastoring in Hawaii for eight
months now. The first few months were great,
but ministry can be like tending a garden —
sometimes the weeds don't show up until later.

About six months into our ministry here, I
became aware of some rumblings, dissatisfaction,
and rumors. A few people even left the church. I
heard that they were angry and didn't feel I was
pastoring as I should. Granted, I still have much
to learn. I am a young pastor, and I will make
more mistakes.

I felt badly for a long time. I tried to reconcile
everyone's differences and change the things I
could but to no avail. Even though I apologized,
it still wasn't enough. People continued to leave
the church. I began to notice a subtle change in
my approach to people. I started to do things to
gain people's favor.

One evening God spoke clearly to my heart,
"You can't be a politician and a pastor." I
understood what He was saying. I had been

trying to please everyone, dodging the pruning shears whenever possible. I had to be confident in my call, teachable in my spirit, and always content to serve an Audience of One.

You see, often God allows things to happen, painful as they might be, in an effort to prune you. Whether it be unwise decisions, unfruitful activities, or even inaccurate perspectives. When you feel pain, it may not be the devil. It may well be God's pruning shears. Cooperate with Him. See His direction and incline your ear to His instructions. Get counsel from God-fearing elders.

> *"Listen to counsel and accept discipline that you may be wise the rest of your days." (Pr. 19:20)*

I learned a great lesson about fruit bearing from a guava farmer in our church. In Hawaii, unlike the mainland, we don't have summer "growing seasons." The reason is that winter's temperatures are somewhat the same as summer's! So I asked the farmer, "When do the guava trees produce guavas?"

His reply was, "They produce guavas just after I prune them."

Always remember, the secret to fruitfulness isn't adding. It's pruning.

> *"Every branch in Me that does not bear fruit, He takes away; and every branch that bear fruit, He prunes it, that it may bear more fruit!" (John 15:2)*

I can't explain to you the peace that God gave me when I finally resolved that conflict. It's God's church. He said that He would build it and I will not stand in His way nor try to compete with Him. If I want to be a "fruit-bearing" tree in the kingdom, I'd better plan on getting pruned. When I think of the flavorful fruit He will bring, I can then release Him to prune my character, my ministry, my relationships, and my activities.

> *"I am the true vine, and My Father is the vinedresser. Every branch in Me that does not bear fruit, He takes away; and every branch that bears fruit, He prunes it, that it may bear more fruit." (John 15: 1-2)*

Yielded to the shears,
Dad

*G*ems for
Motivation

What Really Counts

*Look for God's applause and not
the world's.*

Dear Aaron,

This morning you made a picture in Sunday School for me. You color very interestingly and your imagination is great! However, I loved your gift not because of your impeccable "artwork," but because you are my child. It was my relationship with you that brought worth to the artwork. It was precious because it came from my son.

Although the Lord gives us many opportunities to serve Him, our performance does not determine our position with Him. Rather, our position gives worth to our performance. God doesn't applaud us on the basis of our results or successes. He applauds us on the basis of relationship! We are His kids!

You also did a somersault for me last night. To be honest, it wasn't the best one I've ever seen. You almost broke your neck! And even though you hit the wall (you ran out of space because you didn't start in the middle of the room), you still stood proudly when I clapped for you. You enjoyed the applause because you did your best and felt my love and approval.

Some days you will feel as if there's nothing you can do correctly. During those times, please don't compare your performance to others or feel that you have to succeed to gain love and acceptance. I love you because you are my son, and I am honored because Jesus let me be your dad. Rest in that, and when you do, you'll notice things getting better and better.

Look for God's applause and not the world's. Soon, you'll be producing masterpieces. You'll do spectacular somersaults! But always remember what brings value to all we do for God. The value is not in what we produce. What we produce is made valuable by our relationship with Him!

> Applauding wildly,
> Dad

Fulfillment

Keep your heart eternal -
Seeing beyond the physical and
into the everlasting.

My dear son Aaron,

Right now I'm cruising toward Seattle at 30,000 feet. When I left Eugene, Oregon, it was terribly rainy and stormy. But up here, the skies are blue and beautiful. The sun is so bright that I can't even look outside the plane at times. What a contrast from the gray, dismal weather down below.

Although I enjoy the sunshine, the service of the flight attendant and the seats are fairly comfortable, this isn't where my ministry is. It's down there in the rainy, stormy city — that's where the people are. That's where I will ultimately be the happiest and most fulfilled.

Unfortunately, many people think comfort equals happiness. That isn't always true. Don't get fooled by that. Some think that being financially independent is the greatest goal in life. You must live for something much greater than comfort. Money cannot buy fulfillment. It might buy a companion, but it can never buy love. It can buy a house, but it can never buy a home. It can buy feelings, but it will never buy faithfulness.

Jesus bore the cross for me, and that was terribly uncomfortable. But that was the only place in the world where He could say, "It is finished." He had fulfilled His Father's call, and He was fulfilled as well.

Always keep your eyes on the right goals, Aaron. Be sure of your race and your direction. Recalibrate often back to the cross, otherwise you'll end up setting your heart on the wrong things.

I have run four marathons so far. I'd like to do a few more. The most memorable was the second one. A friend and I ran together, but we didn't train very well that year. We procrastinated, and a month before the race, we made up our minds to go for it. The day came and filled with adrenaline and good intentions, we started off. At about twenty-two miles, we hit the famous invisible membrane stretched across every runner's' path called "The Wall." This is a point in the race where your body is depleted and everything in you wants to shut down. But like troopers, we kept going. Our feet felt like we were running on a hot bed of coals. My lungs were on fire, and it felt like someone was stabbing each thigh with a knife each time my Nikes collided with the pavement.

Rounding the final corner, in the distance, we could see that some balloon company had put up a huge rainbow of colored balloons that arched the finish. We could see it from a quarter mile away. My partner who was as depleted as I was, set his heart to make it at least to the balloons! Everything in him was geared to not collapse till AFTER the balloons! But what we didn't know was that the balloons weren't at the finish line! It was yet another fifty yards further!

When we came to the balloons and my partner noticed that it wasn't the finish line, he just about died on the spot. It took everything in me to convince him to keep running just a little further. If you look at the picture of that year's finish, you'll see us helping each other over the finish line!

Be sure you're not running toward colorful balloons, Aaron. Make sure your goals are godly and accurate. They won't always involve comfort, status, popularity or ease. These things are temporary. Keep your heart with an eternal perspective — seeing beyond the physical to the everlasting. Don't get fooled into thinking that you can cruise at 30,000 feet all the time and be happy. Your true fulfillment is with your feet on the ground, sleeves rolled up, and running THROUGH the colored balloons to the finish!

Setting my heart in the right place,
Dad

Because of Relationship

God isn't looking for super saints.
He's looking for true children.

Dear Amy,

We were invited to your preschool Christmas program. Although you're only three years old, your class was going to sing some Christmas carols to the parents. You weren't really excited to perform because you had lost a couple of your front teeth and you didn't want people to see your toothless grin. But after some prodding, you decided to overlook the absent teeth and sing anyway.

The evening came, and your mom and I, armed with a flash camera and full of expectancy, headed for the concert. The room was packed with proud parents, all prepared with the same idea of capturing a Kodak moment.

Your class, about 30 or so, filed onto a three-tiered riser, each donned with a red cape and glitter in their hair. Your teacher, with guitar slung over her shoulder, was the sole director for this three-year-olds' Christmas extravaganza.

When everyone was ready and in their places, she began to strum the beginning chords to "Joy to the World." After the first chord, I knew she had forgotten something . . . to tune her guitar! But the discordant clash of melody didn't seem to phase her in the least.

With a broad smile, she signaled the singers to begin. With toothless effort, the children began . . . but not to sing. They began calling out to their parents, uncles, and families. While the teacher lifted her voice to lead, the children were more interested in being noticed!

"Hi Mom! Hi Dad! Here I am!"

And the teacher continued her solo, "Joy to the world!"

One of the boys began to fall backwards off the risers and bravely took two others with him. The teacher continued her discordant solo, "Joy to the world!" You couldn't find us so you sat down and started to cry. The teacher paused, a bit distracted by all the commotion, but quickly regained her composure and continued her solo debut, "Joy to the world!"

It was chaotic! But when the final note ended (Praise the Lord), there was a spontaneous standing ovation! Flash cameras whirred continually snapping frame after frame to capture the moment on film. We were all such proud parents.

But in the midst of this battery-driven flash-storm, I was caught by a passing thought. I wondered with all the chaos, flat guitar, and falling bodies, why in the world did I ever give a standing ovation to one of the worst concerts I've ever attended? We even took time to capture this on film!

But then I caught something . . . I realized that we didn't applaud on the basis of the performance. Why did we applaud? It sure wasn't the quality of music or movement. We applauded because those were our kids! It really had little to do with performance. It had everything to do with relationship!

And that doesn't only go for me. That's how God feels about you too. He applauds you not on the basis of your performance. He loves and applauds you because you're His child!

Relationship. That's what's most precious to the Lord. And as we walk in a genuine relationship with Him, any small attempt to please Him becomes something beautiful to God. He's not looking for super saints. He's looking for true children.

Then when we do sing, all of heaven applauds ... regardless of how we sound!

Joy to the World!
Dad

What Satisfies You?

*Chaff can fill you for awhile, but
it can never satisfy your heart.*

Dear Abby,

Whenever I am traveling, Mom let's you sleep in the bed with her. But when I return, you have to go back to your own bed. Sorry.

I had been traveling in Japan for about ten days, so you got a bit too comfortable sleeping in our room. When bedtime came, I tucked you comfortably under your "Cinderella" covers, and I headed off to bed. I was somewhere between slumber and sleep when I felt this "presence" staring at me in the dark. I was startled awake only to find you standing there looking at me.

"Can I sleep in the bed with you?"

"No. Dad's home, so you get to sleep in your own bed."

"But I missed you."

"Well, I'm home now, and I'll be in the same house as you all night, so go to bed."

I marched you back to your bedroom, and after tucking you back under the covers, I returned once more to bed. It wasn't more than five minutes when you appeared a second time.

"Can I sleep in your bed with you just for tonight? I'm scared to be alone."

I explained that the Lord was with you and you had nothing to worry about. Then you offered option two: "Then can I sleep on the floor next to your bed?"

"No," I said. "I paid good money for your bed, so I want you to make use of it." I marched you back to your room, and to discourage any future returns, I locked the bedroom door and fell fast asleep.

I usually get up earlier than anyone else to do my devotions, so at 5 o'clock, I got dressed and started for the kitchen. When I opened the bedroom door, I stumbled over a heap of blankets, a pillow, a teddy bear and a little girl curled up just outside the bedroom door. Your little body had been pressed against the door all night, content and fast asleep. The hard floor wasn't a deterrent to your desire to be close.

I picked you up and put you on my side of the bed next to your sleeping mom. My heart just about burst with love for you as I thought about you sleeping on the hard floor. It was then that the Lord spoke gently to my heart and reminded me that what should satisfy each of us was so clearly shown in you. Even though the floor was hard and the night was chilly, you were satisfied. The cold tile of the hallway floor was unnoticeable compared with being close to Mom and Dad.

That's how I want to be with Jesus. When I am close to Him, I am satisfied.

A lot of things will vie for your attention. Chaff can fill you for awhile, but it will never satisfy your heart. Material possessions, relationships, and other things will be advertised as that which will satisfy you. I remember some years ago, an iced tea commercial touted how a certain brand, "Ah, satisfies you." Even chewing tobacco joined the team of products promising satisfaction. But for the child of God, only one thing satisfies, and Psalms 65 reminds us of what that is.

> *"How blessed is the one whom Thou dost choose, and bring near to Thee, to dwell in Thy courts. We will be satisfied . . ." (Psalm 65:4)*

Stay close to Jesus, and when you are, the temptations for other things will have no hold over you. You'll be so satisfied that other lures will pale in comparison to the joy of being close to Jesus. And when you are close to Him, you find, quite unlike me, the Lord will open His door wide to His child and welcome you in!

Learning from your heart,
Dad

About the Author

Wayne Cordeiro is presently the Senior Pastor of New Hope Christian Fellowship in O'ahu, a new work that was planted in September, 1995. In its first four years, New Hope grew to over 6,000 at weekend services with 4,800 receiving Christ for the first time. New Hope O'ahu is currently listed as one of the fastest growing churches in the nation.

Prior to moving to O'ahu, Pastor Wayne was the Senior Pastor at New Hope Christian Fellowship in Hilo, Hawaii for almost 12 years.

He has also planted 20 other churches in Hawaii, Guam, and Japan. Wayne was raised in Palolo Valley on O'ahu and lived in Japan for three years. He then moved to Oregon where he finished his schooling and ministry training over the next 20 years. In 1975, he graduated Cum Laude from Eugene Bible College and continued graduate studies at Northwest Christian College and the University of Oregon. He served in Youth for Christ for seven years and as a staff pastor at Faith Center in Eugene, Oregon for another three years before returning to Hawaii.

Pastor Wayne is a published songwriter, has released four albums and is a contributing author for church leadership textbooks. He is heard on several radio stations in Hawaii and travels extensively throughout Hawaii, the Mainland U.S., and Internationally to speak at conferences, churches, civic gatherings, prisons, high school assemblies, business forums and leadership conventions.

He is currently writing two other books: "_Dream Releasers_ and _Kingdom Imagineers_."

Pastor Wayne and his wife, Anna, have three children, Amy, Aaron, and Abigail.

For further resources by Wayne Cordeiro, please contact:

New Hope Christian Fellowship O'ahu
290 Sand Island Access Rd.
Honolulu, Hawaii 96819
www.newhope-hawaii.org